D0063627

Into Africa,
Being Black

Books by Fred Lee Hord (Mzee Lasana Okpara)

Poetry
After Hours
Life Sentences: Freeing Black Relationships
Straight Wobblings of My Father

Nonfiction
Reconstructing Memory: Black Literary Criticism
I Am Because We Are (coeditor with Jonathan S. Lee)
Black Culture Centers: Politics of Survival and Identity (editor)

Into Africa, Being Black
New and
Selected Poems

Fred Lee Hord
(Mzee Lasana Okpara)

Foreword
Haki R. Madhubuti

THIRD WORLD PRESS
Progressive Black Publishing Since 1967
Chicago

Third World Press
Publishers since 1967
Chicago

© 2013 by Fred Lee Hord.

All Rights reserved. No part of the material protected by this copyright
notice may be reproduced, stored in a retrieval system, or transmitted in
any form by any means, electronic mechanical, photocopying, recording
or otherwise without prior written permission, except in the case of brief
quotations embodied in critical articles and reviews. Queries should be sent
via e-mail to: twpress3@aol.com or Third World Press, P.O. Box 19730,
Chicago, IL 60619.

First Edition
Printed in the United States of America.

Library of Congress Control Number: 2013944785

ISBN 13: 978-0-88378-349-8

Cover designer and illustration: Lori Reed
Author photograph: Magali Roy Fequiere
Interior designer: Solomohn N. Ennis-Klyczek

to

Terry Lee Duffy

Contents

Straight Wobblings of My Father

Into Africa, Being Black

On Mission: The Poetry and Work of Fred Lee Hord

Here between these covers, printed on almost one hundred and eighty pages, transferred from the handwritten manuscript is a life's work in poems. Dr. Mzee Fred Lee Hord's poetry spans over forty years of a purposed and contemplative life. Though *Into Africa, Being Black: New and Selected Poems* is not an autobiography, in reading Dr. Hord's poetry, we read a history of well-defined literary, political, academic, and personal struggle.

I first met Fred Lee Hord in the early 1970s when I visited Franklin College in Indiana. He approached me with his first manuscript of poetry, *After(h)ours.* Third World Press published his book along with a series of books from five others poets whom we designated as First Poets. The First Poets included Angela Jackson, Sandra Royster, and Chester Fuller. These poets were precocious, on fire, full of Black optimism, and ready for the struggle then and to come. Out of all of them, Fred Hord stood out to me as a young man committed to his people beyond the ordinary. He was on a mission that he was still defining. He writes in "An Ace So Black, He's Royal":

> a man is not the sum of the eyes on him
> nor his inner laughter the buy of sweet pearls;
> he is as tall as what he stands up for,
> and as strong as the give of his world.

Part of his mission was to earn his PhD and to teach. However, there was something in him eating at his soul that few would imagine coming from this poet, this scholar of our literature. For those in the know, he comes off as a quiet, brilliant thinker, a creative hurricane who always sees beyond the stifling walls of white nationalism and white supremacy. In him was a calling burning out of control that freed him to think and act beyond prescribed boxes. In Dr. Hord's poetry, he manifests his own destiny and captures the musical and melodious tones of liberation. This is clarified in "After(h)ours," the title poem of his first collection:

> Fitting our lives flush with each other,
> we work through shifts of strategic leisure

making constant the collective example
for those whose after(h)ours are still for one.

His articulation and founding of the National Association for Black Culture Centers in 1988 incorporated him into the history of our people, of our culture, and into America's consciousness. This was an extraordinary endeavor that demanded a commitment that few poets or artists of any discipline are willing to make, much less carry out. His journey has been extraordinary and demanding, requiring a critical part of his life and the life of his family. Let me be clear, to build Black institutional structures outside of the mainstream is actually an act of revolution to which few scholars of African Studies have given any serious thought. He forecasts his future in the poem "Black Time":

> when it comes my time
> to pray my time
> while the young I've taught scream
> and sing martial songs;
>
> I will not bide my time
> in warm rocking chairs
> or cool porch swings
> or sweet memories

Dr. Hord's poetry is socio-political commentary as well as an emergency call to recognize the importance of Black/African culture; a conscious love song undeterred by his people's self hatred and ignorance. He views art of all genres as an answer and a question. His contribution to poetry and the poetic form is on serious display in this collection. In poems like "Wish I Were Your Perfect Rhyme," "Words," and "Quilting Races Together," we read a poet on course to cement his legacy of excellent writing within messages that honor his history, culture, and people. He is keenly aware of the downtime that African Americans are experiencing at this historical moment. He is intellectually cognizant of most of the statistics measuring our current decline. He is not a romantic, but a sensitive realist. His concern is apparent in "Valleys in Mountaintops":

> King did not live long enough
> to see swelling armies march backward

to American dreams of more empty stuff,
with some Black soldiers shooting to lie in front
or least hold up the crumbling rear.

He would warn newest mercenaries
their belly commitment to one per cent
puts them in the eye of final storms
more deadly than hunger, segregation or chain
that will send them flat under knees
where even prayers cannot be sent.

In a world sadly in need of change, in need of a revolutionary makeover, he chose to reshape business and culture. Dr. Hord rewrote the struggle manual for academics and students in founding the National Association for Black Culture Centers. He and his colleagues were interested in helping students work toward success. They did this by combating the isolation and unacknowledged invisible shunning that Black students experience. They were particularly invested in making sure that African American students had access to professional mentoring and examples of serious Black men and women in the academy. They created intellectual and cultural brick and mortar centers throughout the nation where students could escape to, seek refuge, and not feel like "the other."

Most of all, the members feared that without an institutional response to white nationalism and supremacy in the academy, students would be consumed by Eurocentricism and graduate more confused and consciously whiter than they were when they entered the world of higher education. Their study of Western tradition—or to put it more effectively, white studies— ruled the day. In fact, like the battle for Black Studies, the struggle for the National Association for Black Culture Centers is an uplifting story. Dr. Hord is always the voice to proclaim the critical importance of African heritage, bonding traditions, and history. He gives no quarter to those who argue against his efforts. I have an internal smile in my heart for him.

He is able to write, teach, and organize at a national level. As a poet he understands intuitively the determinative force of culture. Black/African culture represented the underpinning of a self-reliant people fully aware of their place in the international world of real politics. He writes in "Returning Home,"

As Africans, we should have known
everything loved needs to return

. . . .

Everything loved will return.

This precious volume of new and selected poems justly widens
Dr. Hord's space among the poets of the Black Arts Movement. He
remains, as John O. Killens would state, one of the long distance
runners. He is in a league with Amiri Baraka, Sonia Sanchez, Askia
Toure, Jayne Cortez, Eugene B. Redmond, Lucille Clifton, Kalamu
ya Salaam, and others who created a movement that helped to change
America and the world for the literate and liberated majority. As he
writes of Malcolm X, he reflects—as I read it—on his own life.

You, carpenter of solid dreams,
tall as you needed to be
to see life and look death in the eye;
no dunce caps or leashes for you
nor chaining pats on your head
where once had been the lye.

Yes, as a cultural son of Malcolm X, he has been able to actualize
in words and actions what that awesome movement offered. As poet
and institution builder, he remains first among the clear geniuses of
our culture. I call him friend, brother, and family of the word and
more.

Haki R. Madhubuti

After(h)ours

After(h)ours

After(h)ours is our joint,
not a white girl's big black dream
nor a twisted cigarette (double negative)
nor a place to party pale till light

but a work connection
smoking black dreams to fire.

Our joint is not a matter of imagined inches
and the mile scream of mouths without men,
for we do not start and end below the belt.

Our joint is not a matter of roll your own
and the individual highs beneath the smoke,
for we are rising above the weed together.

Our joint is not a matter of one bulb suns
and the two-day fun we could nod together,
for a nation holds more freedom than weak ends.

After(h)ours is our joint.

Fitting our lives flush with each other,
we work through shifts of strategic leisure
making constant the collective example
for those whose after(h)ours are still for one.

Black Seed

Falling off the tree
when I was green,
I mellowed on the ground.

I wait now,
watching brothers on the limb
turn from the sun

or sprawl under shades
to avoid their ripening.

Too many brothers
rot in high places
without ever entering
the mouth of their history.

I want only to be found,
picked up,
and give flavor to black life.

Everything begins and ends at seed.

I would rather be
       trampled
than
out
of
        reach!

Full Grown Pain

Pain paints eyes red
It drives a hand across a cheek
It turns volume up to screaming
It forces feet out the door

Black men have run around years in a day
to be free from the torturing crawl of tomorrows

What has happened to a man
who will let the hurt color his eyes in wine
bend precious faces with his hands
yell at ears he has kissed
and leave people he has asked to come

Your hurt is still young enough to master,
still small enough to lift and
still warm enough to flow

Your daddy's pain was too old to
give lessons to
too heavy to boost up
and too cold to pass.

We Have Been Men

From infant screaming
to adult dry tears,
from late milk bottles
to early wine ones,
from the snot
and our handkerchief tongues
to the stench
our noses forgot,
from rags that wiped up
only a little cold
to those that made us hot
in other eyes,
from marbles to losing everything
because the circle was removed,
from the strangeness of our fathers
to the strangeness of our sons,
from our mothers' knees
to our own,
from the first spanking
to the last mind whipping,

we have been men.

We have grown up on the crawl
to be men, for white boys,
who could only walk in basinets,
who could only work sitting down,
who could only love in fairy tales,
could not stand their slaves as men.

We have heard the words of love
shouted backwards to rhythms of hate,
we have played the dozens
to bully the spirit of Virgin Mary,

we have played hide and seek
with food that would never be it,
we have shot pool
on the only carpet in our lives,
we have instructed
dancing crap in the streets,
and danced our pain
into bystanding.

We have strutted and limped
because sick people were walking straight,
we have marched on waterbugs
and fenced with rats,
we have buried the ears of baby sisters,
erecting popsicle tombstones.

We have missed our fathers so much
we couldn't find them when they came home,
and drunk our mothers' tears
and the soup she stretched with faucet rivers.
We have offered new cheeks to her anger
when she has been laid for our getting up,
and glorified the orphaned foods
she could then bring home.

And
we have lied more truthfully in barber shops
than dreams did at night,
we have taken the wine
in the name of our blood,
we have loved Saturday night
for the wonderful segregation of its joys,
and loved our churches
for being the afterset.

And even though,
we have lied to our women
because truth had no language,
and have sold our absences
for food and rent,
and have bragged of our babies
to season everyday humility,
and worn our do's and wigs
to straighten the kink of forever,
and bleached our skin
to clean the white stain,
and killed our brothers
because they were safer than the enemy,

we have always been men.

And now that the machines
have lost their minds,
and their green creatures
have burned them out,
we will handle the world
with craftsmanship again,

for we have been men.

Life Sentences

Life Sentences

I cried
and you kicked;
you cried
and I ran tongue
over jagged teeth,
filing for the kill.

Africa, white beginning.
Our trial
their trailings
our sentencing
their chains.
Parting waters.

Iron,
which we freed first
was shaped to bend us,
to lock us in linear looplets,
to leave us flat alone,
yet we kept the circle,
generations short of breath
feeling the pulse to be free.

Our eyes were soft orbits,
touches gentle;
we wept for each other more than ourselves.
Standing straight,
we surrounded spaces of love.

We faced our custody
in each other's arms,
unborn children stirring us
with promises of their deeds.

We laughed at light bars
that held our silhouettes.

Life sentences.
New generations felt closed
by windows in supple stone
open to diamond catacombs,
seeing without our caked blood.

We had fenced them less
with old stories,
yet turning their eyes,
they found freedom in black cells,
laughing at gates on all sides
before the bounties.

Then,
crooked fingers became the key,
invitations of feasts, leisure, and panoply.
They wanted,
their bellies were full of empty;
they wanted,
their backs and necks were broken;
they wanted,
love seemed shabby,
too hard to dress up.

We no longer struggle together.
We no longer lie
to get up and fight.
We want to be.
We want to be them.
We want to be free
of the fragment lines
that crisscross
small wedged openings.

Life sentences.
Although
we know the heave of breathing
is not the rhythm of soul,
that the spirit is safe
from ghoully power and disease,
that final entrapment means
our consent to be shut in,
most arise unfaithfully,
turning our backs to
the love we made
against the wall.

The living rest
must right our freedom,
living love songs,
returning home
with African spirit
without blame or anger
to the eyes and hands
that held us best,
writing new sweet blues
to keep us one.

Prize Apart

These last few years,
our sisters' cries
of life and love without us
have turned my ear inside.

And I have reckoned why
we spit in each other's eye
or walk politely new poles apart,
too nice to mar the race in light.

We have suffered and prospered to forgetting.
The griot is silent in such haze,
and we cannot hear above the noise
of blame and promised praise.

Recompense

There are sins white as death
and almost as long,
violations of the head and heart
and the tearing of our limbs

when we pulled at the pantlegs
of the monsters who trampled the earth

in order to sit on you.

Claiming last names and last words,
first sons and (hy)mens,
we have boasted of our crimes
as the sign of health.

We come now in the only time
with fists empty of splintering,
with silence and ears in our bones
to beg some eye of concern
that you have kept covered
in our assault.

Your late screams and loud remembering
have wrestled us from the muscling nightmare,
the dream of the left side of God,
the required crawling to the throne.

We come on our knees,
having forgotten the balance of erection,
willing to work new terms,
to wait the shaking of the hands.

We do not need to feel tall again,
but shall find a way to stand with you.

The He'll of My Dancing Dust

Black is forever.
In the grip of ancestors,
you learn how to live in it,
how to breathe back the flames far enough
to lick and bless the fire.

I stoked the heat
with eyes and passionate speech.
I straightened the curves I love,
angling what was round and sacred.

I did not blame myself at first.
It was the movement of wondrous globes,
the rhythms of their circularities that enchanted,
spelling my spellboundedness.

When coupled with hot frontal worlds
that gazed back,
I forgot the ancient Egyptian warning
the picture in the river
may tell on you
without your best self.

And although it was joining
that I craved,
I multiplied them,
dividing too much soul in pools.

Not claiming love when lying,
I yet subjected all spirits
to object in consenting,
and so I burned for years.

I kept shrinking
even as I reduced faces
who proudly filed to unmarked places
to be filled and emptied again.

The flint of such fleshings
blew and banked a smoldering
that soon leaped
to scorch my eyes
and leave only
the charred spaces of my desire
to see all women through.

Then I met you,
too late to reclaim clear sight.
Each time I watched you
through the eyes of what you felt,
I caught reflections of the spiraling,
heard the whisperings and moanings
of missing meaning.

Each sweet softness I had known
baked stone now or turned to ashes;
I saw you only through the fire.

We separate,
slipping away
on muddy banks we have poured,
parched inside.

It is he'll,
a self-made construction;
black street corner icon,
soul lost in the flesh
I thought my own.

Sick and Tired of This Mesh

I think I have known
for some time now
in the forty years of wandering
trying to make women my home.

I think I have known
in the fist of my groin,
I could not hammer out loins
and be at peace with them.

I think, I think I have known
that the semen from my eyes
may melt in several bones
but leave me all alone.

I am not a woman
so can never know
or remember the pod,
nine months of feeling God.

I buck and whinny,
heave and start
in the twinkling of a heaven
which spends me back to earth,

and even when I wear
pure vestments of the mind,
I find my testicles in hand
and am pocketed from my love.

What can I do in my hungering
to keep the humping in this pit,
to savor the stretched out fit
of being two places at one?

I am African and man,
reared twice at once in this land,
set on the knees of ancient times,
spread on my knees to ride the myth.

I am over tired of this,
and need a kiss to keep past lips
to clutch the touch through work days
and at least two changings of the season.

Wish I Were Your Perfect Rhyme

I must leave.
I am not man enough to stay.
I need back what I gave away
before I loved you in your mountains.

My strength
I shot and dribbled down canyons.
My hair is gone.
I cannot push the pillar up.

I need you to cuddle my head
till my stubble curls grow strong,
and I shall be afraid if you leave me long
till I see my muscle in your eyes.

I wonder if someone had shown
when I first opened curlilocks and yellow face
to make the heart of a woman race,
that tallies slice inside when you mark the wall,

if I might still have pushed full steam ahead,
or if instead I would have raised my sites
to where loving makes triphammering right,
and keep the ripple in my mind.

I do not know,
but maybe the question in my eyes
when little black boys discussed their lies
left me prone to too many ans(hers),

for in the center of my laugh, I found a poem
and in the pupil of my tears, I found a poem,
but the brine ran down to purse the lips
that I forced open jaggedly for your kiss.

I want to be a poem with you.
Perhaps if I had not given spring of my rhyme
to young sticky snows in summertime,
I might rise and fall with you in cadence.

Middle Class Black Man

Yesterday, I was blue
and you were putatively
in the pink
because I supported you
on the pedestal.

Day before,
we stayed in the red
for being black
to white slaves
who could not level,
much less lift their eyes.

Today,
I should know better twice
than to act male or white,
for I have lived with you
under the heel
squirming for soft, not steel.

Yet sometimes,
as you may find with child,
this world that teaches up and down
and not around
tempts you to the top
to keep from falling off.

Tonight,
help me prepare for dawn
by pressing my muscle down,
meshing sinew with soul.
I want strength to be gentle,
be touch enough to share.

Small Town Links

It was simple at first.

You and I,
woman and man,
black and black,
old enough to know how to act
would mock the loneliness
of this small white town.

That was all.

We would honor ancient forces,
wink at the seasons,
handling our own green and heat,
and talk about black writers
when the pulse cooled.

We would be friends too,
not just in the month's red edges
or the gray of distance,
but be the other ear.

We would shake hands
in our fire.
But somehow
in the celebration
of sharing this space,
in free laughter about the luck of it,
in the exuberance of new arms that fit,
even in the quieting of old echoes,
we forgot the mystery,
that same and other side of magic,
the strange counting of feeling,
that touching may not reach love
but is never plain.

Everybody grown knows these things.

Our first fight
should have opened us,
roughed up our satin hands,
leaving our whisperings more precious.

The first slammed door
should have cracked our dream,
or the telephone clicks
left longer silences.

Our droughts,
when tears were not enough
for me to grow
or even your earth to plant me
should have meant
winters too long for spring,
but we played misty,
gloved our hands,
and screamed four-letter words
above the din.

We even brought wine
to water the soil,
adding apologetic gifts of black writers.

Last night was plain again.
Let us be the stars
that were not there
to see that it is over,
to ask if it ever began.
Let us settle for whatever poems
the small town links have allowed
and choose our freedom.

Tough Losses

Black men cry too.

For seven years I have watched you,
unlucky lover,
too black to let day light in
when dark was our peoples' way to win.

Your fists were too tight
for anything but soft to seep out;
you held enemies with the smile
that kept us standing.

"I am the shock troops."

You mixed that favorite line
with visions of my words advancing
after you took the ground.

The air sometimes needs pounding
when it is too thick to breathe,
and your palms out closed
might have protected you for a while.

But you wanted to knock down
and pick up with one hand
in the same motion. With the other,
you tied heart behind your back.

Black men cry too.

We lose women.
We lose jobs.
We lose appendages.
We lose the wild of voice.

The heart does not beat right
with these skippings,
but strength is to laugh
and cry at such irregularities.

Talk to slave husbands
about the awful crowd of three.
Listen to sharecropper questions
about account in loved one's eyes.

Sit on stone with old urban fighters
who lost precious smiles in fickle machines,
or on ice with hands that speak
their uselessness, losing soft fingers.

It did not start with you.
It is not just that we lose when we try.
Black fists do not hide power well
enough to escape the metal.

I have cried too,
at the back of a woman,
in front of her questions,
near her sleeping side.

I know tough losses.

Sometimes, I speak callouses.

I am not ashamed to cry for you.

I shall cry with you only long enough
to talk you back
into taking on the world again.

Coming Off a High

I don't need tables anymore
for my hands to rule,
nor a throne of sky for my head,
nor double my laughter
to double my fun,

nor my eyes doubling their centers
to expand the world,
nor sweat that changes heat
when I'm alone.

I need to reach straight for you
to build the power of our trembling.
I need to feel earth
under the toes, balls, heels of my feet
while I help seek our stars.

I need pieces of quiet
to fit our laughter.
I need to point my eyes at yours
to share the point of ours
as we keep the waters of our love
warm forever.

As Tall As a Man

Perhaps I'm growing.

For long moments, I stunted myself,
because I saw myself as short,
using the single eye
of old young cut down black men

who turned from African measures of men,
learning such dimensions were not tall
in the new world, and were shown no way
that standing straight would lend stature.

I was a giant in the new world
but saw my height as dwarf.
Money is paper, after all,
and many stand out who crawl.

So I turned to brothers on the block
before close enough to see their size,
and learned secrets, laughing and loud,
of keeping your heads in the clouds.

Some wisdom frightened me, though;
potions to make your bass grow,
piercing your arm for muscle,
eating powder through the nose;

and I did not understand the wobble,
nor sleeping in the broad of day,
nor seeing only some forever
that left friends up close far away.

Yet women looked ripe in that world,
and the men had picked them all,
and magic stories on magic corners
were jeers at failure and feeling small.

Trying to forget mother and two sisters
and the man of cloth whose words of girls
were steel sermons in my room,
I joined that tiptoe flexing world.

I sprang up overnight,

old pencil marks
on kitchen door casing
at the top of my straining head
now just bad memories.

I backed to inner mirrors though

for a big boy while
in this new measuring,
and looked instead through
the smiles of women looking up.

But the father who was polished glass
became a clear wall everywhere,
and I could not grow past tot,
with each new pair of arms propping me up.

"Treat her like she was your sister"
was the real ruler over my head,
and I could no longer shrink
beneath his favorite sermon and proud eyes.

Airlines: To a Black Stewardess

The images crowded in your form
and led you up the cabin aisle.

Face of dreams, eyes to keep you awake,
perfect teeth to nibble your tongue,
hair to towel you dry,
and a smile to swallow the girl back home.

Wound-up dolls fleshing in the air,
legs spread for nasty heights
squeezing you down to size below
or in a quiet corner of the sky.

Then you turned and locked me in
with one look and tug of your small hands,
and I could not catch my breath
or find a way to take my head
out of the clouds with you.

For your eyes held no three-letter answers
nor your smile a promise to give me ground,
and I knew a night was not enough
to make room enough to share.

Out of the color they require,
you wear more gracefully your own.
You seem comfortable in black,
able to work without white aprons,
a lovely host for our history.

But,
I listen to your turbulence,
how some flights have forced you down,
how each time you wait longer

to try your wings again,
and I wonder when or if
you will work to fly with me.

I, too, have ridden troublesome air
and sought the land
to fill the pockets of my life,
but I cannot get to love on time
by advancing sure steps alone.

I shall risk new space with you
and chart its course inside;

keep your wings,
but let me cover your heart.

Definitions

Pants and skirts,
inverted triangles and curves;
such are the definitions.

Pink and blue,
tears and sinew,
such are the definitions.

Although my pants do not need the belt,
and my soul is cinched soft by suffering,
and I don pink shirts with black bottoms,
and cry so easily at muscling,

I know how these designs murder.

Yet add the mix
of American man and manners
to Othello, who is also Caliban,
and African love seems buried.

A man is what he amounts to
and what he mounts.
Measure his manhood by the size
of his mansion, meals, and meanness
and the tenderness he straddles.

And if he is black
and boy till death
yet not the old boy,
and can climb on no heads
to build his mansion
or see his meals,
he is no count.

If that does not sour him enough
to tuck his head between his legs and walk,
boasting of that contortion,
he may also watch his eyes hate
and betray the African in his face
he finds in mirrors under him.

This poem is
for the woman whose horizontal gaze
is a bridge for our understanding,
who wears pants
where my skills are short skirts,
and stands an erect soldier
putting strong shoulders to our wheel,
whose blues make mine pastel,
yet lend large daring to my spirit.

After the Tears, Our Years

Although I weep with you
about the lack of us,
the more than many men who turn
numbers back on heels,

who, full of poison,
fill prisons with barrels in their back,
or turn their backs
for sisters and daughters of the guardians

or the back alleys of boys,
mixing guns in large death ways;
or who spin Sam's ransomed steel
to kill their reflections in the world;

although I break down
at your funerals which are our wedding,
and want to softly be a brother
until hard times are history or better,

I wince in my own brine.
Black women on the want in my wounds,
without question marks in dollar signs
add zeroes to the sacred words;

or the salt of rivals with fair eyes,
wide hips, or jolly giants
who muscle in sweet whisperings.
Boy, you read too many books.

So, I cry with you lonely ladies
while looking through my tears
to find one of you
looking for a man who works his love.
Numbers are no measure of sweethearts
free from machines spinning the world;
those pretty African lovers who are won
by might, money, and such meridians

are no more available than brothers
behind bars, freebasing in chosen cells,
caressing calluses and codpieces
or in other early hells.

Wherever you are,
wipe away the tears with me
and walk with clear vision
toward the sound of our union.

If you meet a man
before we reach each other,
who needs you to be strong with him
to carry more burden of our people,

who needs you to be tall with him
to see tomorrow above the burden,
and who needs you to share books with him
to piece the puzzle of your work

even as you lie and fit together,
it is still the sound of our union;
for it is a spirit that you join
and I am only one who carries it.

The numbers we must count with dry eyes
are those who love themselves enough
to love the rest of us in deed,
to multiply those figures in the future.

In an unwhimpering past,
the ancestors chose our other halves.
They do yet when we respect
the loving legacy of their labor.

Black Daddy

Without a model,
how could you know
but to yell at him?

With large hands
only in young dreams,
how could you remember
the soft of muscle?

Go back before his leave
to daddies who filled
the hungry smiles
of small black boys.

For life is tough
in the underbrush.
If blind heads trip your feet,
you will never be a path to manhood.

Even Your Daddy Gets Gray

You saw me before I saw you,
"cute" colored boy with curls
twisting every which way but loose.

You saw me with a rubber ball at two,
world in my small hands,
standing on a platform to be tall
in short pants and white hightop shoes.

You grew and saw the man;
shipshape fro' black as coal
closing in the face of father,
center of your robust circle

and other kids
whose daddies tapped different front doors
or stayed in dark cellars
to be safe from white bombs.

I stood on erect shoulders of history,
spine steadying bubble in the middle,
trousers too long to kneel in lint,
black combat boots in Sunday School.

But as the angle of your regard
began to shut its mouth,
you kept your own wide open
as I walked through winters
with no snow in my head
till they tied my hands behind my back
for knocking the front doors of power.

Yours had never been the house that Fred built.

Soft hands held hammers and saws
and screwed the bolts into place,
but your bellies got full
of a man with no hands;

all your eyes could see
was the table set the way of the womb,
while I dreamed and drank,
belly full before my eyes.

The color of your mother's hair
became the reflection of my lifeless hands
and the pallor in my head.

You did not know, but each night
I dyed my head to keep its color,
although dry wine washed the split ends
and new hands smudged the roots.

One desperate day
before I could seize my throwaway blade
to defend my face
from the gray it had taken on the chin,

I looked back at myself
and the black that had been
and how it still stubbled through
to frame the white
and how you three showed
no gray matter in the mind,

and I smiled first time since I was broke,
seeing no streaks at the top,
just some strands
caught in the creases of my hands.

Even your daddy gets gray.

Survival of the Fittest

(To a daughter graduating from Harvard)

To climb on heads
and walk over bodies
is no sign of strength
nor rise or line to black freedom.

It is the way of the weak
who need skulls and flesh for their feet,
who need their stamp
upon the bone and breathing of the prone.

You were not born of such spirit,
nor did the strong gentle flexing of home
tighten your muscles past passion
or bending toward the might of all.

You had the arm to wrestle Harvard,
to table his use of the purple corpse
and the jumping of the gun
to flatten the sinew of your soul.

I am proud to have been the man
to pass the power of generation to you,
the thick blood that runs unstopping,
the dream that graves could not hold.

I need you to remember that the fists
that kept me on my feet,
that fended for black folks you knew
were not too calloused to tissue your face;

to believe that the iron guts you saw rust
from the spit in my face by potentates
have been mixed to steel by salt alloys.
Yet my center is as supple as your skin.

I Mark your force, singing Laurels
as you emerge to show the fools of Darwin
that strength is the soft of love.
You have pried green from gray ivy walls.

To climb on heads
and walk over bodies
is no sign of strength
nor rise or line to black freedom.

An Ace So Black He's Royal

(To a son graduating from Evansville)

This town you graced at army age
that made fodder of black boys' balls;
this place of athlete aces in forever holes,
a campus without even colored chalk

was where you would hang hat instead of head,
trading gold of your gift for white paper policy.

This butt of jokes before my grownup facts of life,
of zigzag streets and fenced in crazy people
was where you found the bars of your blackness
the safe retreat from their wise insanity.

I knew the rope you would have to walk,
how slipping the hemp can hang you tight.

I knew how those winking lights and flashing whites
burn holes too deep for filling
while warming the skin to panting sweat
and heating the head to bottom burst.

Mark,

a man is not the sum of the eyes on him
nor his inner laughter the buy of sweet pearls;
he is as tall as what he stands up for,
and as strong as the give of his world.

How does a father explain the arith me tic
of plusses adding to nothing or even less?
The birthmark answers boys use for blanks
can never check with life solutions of men.

You did not need twenty-one for grown.
You passed the end of nerve with gentle means
of holding your mother's spirit in fingertips,
away from the aching callous of work too soon.

For you, there was no on and off the court.
The march was always now, the point the same.
You knew aces were pretty but once in a while
when the practice of your love was beyond return,

and that to toe the Mark and serve and volley
was the stuff of most games
of which men were made.
You are made of good stuff, an ace so black
you pitch purple where royalty is in need.

Mark,

more than ever, there is a call for black kings
to softly wear their scepter and their crown
with queens who await the mix to free their own.
Then, we shall be free to cry and share the throne.

I am not of the line of deep-voiced kings
who muscle in when yielding begs for rule;
I have wanted four-fisted kingdoms to serve
to learn the pain and glory of the natal cord.

Perhaps I would not have worn my belly in
when it was full of not providing bread,
nor crawled on all fives with a high head
if I could have earned a living in the red,

but I have seen the sole and felt its print,
and shall never need mirrors or tales again
to understand the wretched view, or retch
when life is too tight to turn over in dreams.

Though I know there are gutters you must sleep in,
I want the cold and cramp of where I've been
to be so breathing and sensate in your mind,
you'll shiver and coil on high ground.

Yet when you pass skid rows, remember my spine
before the falls and the guts I made steps of
to climb back to meet your image and eyes,
and take what you can use to make your stand.

A sundown town. Evanescent sun, black boy run!
No boy, you ran over them and great white hopes.
You won against the odds. Having to pay you to win,
they add an embossed note that you read and write.

It's over now, and I, who squinted my eyes
and held my breath, stare at the black gown
they tried to scare you with, and laugh freely
as you toss the tassels to all that's right.

Continue to toe the Mark and serve and volley;
it is the stuff of life and of which men are made.
You are made of good stuff, an ace so black
you pitch purple where royalty is in need.

Spelman, Spell Woman

(To a daughter graduating from Spelman)

At the point of the slanted pyramid,
upside down in this land,
sister-brother base level
in skewed new cambridge and Ev(e)ns ville,

you are one of three wedges
into the human cracks of black souls
only a jagged line from closed;
you heal wounds as you pry.

Atlanta of the litany,
my baby in the redneck South,
unstoned head in the clouds,
Spelman, Spell Woman.

Atlanta of the Tiffany,
my baby in black bluevein South
namedropping Africa and freedom,
Spelman, Spell Woman.

Atlantis, under the see,
down under from high places
who think mountains do not breathe
and heaven is a mayor's seat.

My baby,
child Marked in her clear face,
old man T(a)rries everyplace.
Girl look like her Daddy,
Spelman, Spell Woman.

You pushed out ancient,
rounded nose and folds
needing youth to smooth,
not young enough for thin air.

45

You pushed out African,
high black in your yellow,
tightening Shirley Temple curls to top,
dribbling left, shooting right.

And so, my daughter
of the nighttime Mommie kiss,
of your hot kiss of Papa's cloth for Grandmommie,
of our family table bliss;

daughter, reaching back for smiles
like Satch for the high hard one,
learning the upper edges of your mouth
catch best the inside cry;

daughter, daughter, Daddy's face yet not passing,
staring at you in your mirror all alone,
his stumbling sounds cracking glass.

God! What's a basement for?

Daughter, I did not know how to jacket my arm
when it could not throw the fast ball
or even catch the ones at your head.
I thought curves would keep me a man, instead.

Oh, the fresh years in the Maryland mountains
have aired my open skin of both sides,
pulling wish and impotence to healing.
The knot is life and love.

No more turning of the key in your sleep,
doors opening now in only your wide-awake.
The white night is over,
Spell Man, Spell Man.
Never again shall I choose the question
of one space too small for us two.

I have worked in thin air to thicken our blood;
Spell Man, Spell Us.

Spelman, Spell Woman,

you always turned the heads around
and turned two eyes to one,
pushing corners to center
with the middle of your sun.

You arise lovelier than before.
Too rich for light,
you bask in the dark heat
of those who see tomorrow.

Spelman, Spell Woman.

From an African Father

They have almost slipped away,
these years,
your eyes in the house.

While I would stall the stay,
inviting though your footsteps' beat,
I suffer this quarter to close,
persuaded that every space
gives contour to those within.

Tomorrow,
I fancy your figures in the wind,
straight, with bow enough to bend,
so strong you need to lift another end,
moving in the rhythm of raise and reason
in the style of our first home.

You have always known who you were;
you understood all race was joined,
but black was real till color
had no power, glory, forever.

To Black Women

You know you are of the dark,
whether dusk, midnight, or dawn;
you know the curl in your hair
shall be a sign for more straight worlds.

Our love is sure as the large star;
our quarrels and leavings, though real,
ash in our hands. It is already by and by;
we raise smiles from liquid guts of eyes.

Love Before Integration

We do not talk about them much;

perhaps, we do not know
our own great love stories.

Women started sagas
of men struggling to keep one foot on shore.

Women who scurried beside their men
in dark dawns to white fields,
winking between the rows
and drops of sweat
which fell in bottomless bags.

Men who winked at their women
after watching legs pried apart
on dirt cabin floors beside clean children,
catching gushing tears,
gently turning heads around,
quieting their own red thunder.

Men who walked several countries
to find those they jumped the broom with,
taking scientific surveys of thousands
to make the point of their lives.

Women smiling with open arms,
lifting the cropped heads of husbands
returning from last accounts of freedom,
slavery for another year.

Men following north stars again,
women wearing unbought paste rings each day,
keeping their promises golden,

working to be sent for
with spic and span children and prayers.

Couples agreeing to promised lands
to feed and clean the master's children
while they caught the dirty dribbling
of work too near the ground to be white.

Honeyed couples raising dreams together
with their children,
waiting on God, working for gold,
plying soup lines till either came.

We do not talk about them much;

perhaps, we do not know
our own great love stories.

Our Love Ain't Evol

Maybe,
if we had found a way back home
to take the famines that had come
when the earth cried open for wet
and we cried by families
with white tongues from too much sun
till we could smile as one,

maybe if we had found a way
to take the famines and plan for days
when horizontal fire would dry the water of our breath
in the blinking of an eye,

maybe
if we had known
more children of the sun past hunting grounds
formed circles too to wait for rain,
so first were last and last first,
the magic powder Europeans changed
to burst from straight lines
would have never turned us in
against our own.

But our unfamiliar fear did not wash our hands;
this land is full of those bad dreams.

Mirrors everywhere,
we had to keep looking down
to make sure the right wrists were chained
and our spirits had not devoured us.

It started there, a new way to keep from dying,
ice in Africa, cold water for drought of gun.
And on the ships,

whose moving sides were more black flesh,
they cut one band to break the rest,
and a round iron world rolled behind one foot
that pointed the way of alien sounds,
"head nigger in charge,
watch the death for your life."

And in the fields,
carpeted and square,
horizon-cornered and bare,
they struck the links of those tired of soul
and touched strange nerves
that when applied to cold,
pulsed privately.

Then they taught the weary
with the history of some million years
to salute with one free hand
and take all in reach with the one still tied,
and aim bottom claw without the ball
at their high place
over our own prostrate,
while the one yet bound
was shoed to kick around
our hearted kin.

Such was the early hail and shuffle,
but it was not enough
to pit women and men.
Our new reflex was not yet sure enough
for their risking gold pyramids and swelling heads,
nor was their patting of the back
for the poking out of chest
old enough sanction
to lift dark eyes from the ground.

So they followed us to our fires,

the guarded sacred heat of hearth
that we fanned with breath and mind,
and raised their metal pyres
to burn our insides out alive,
and our love was no match sometimes
to light the lips or eyes
in ashes of those sights
or memories.

Memory is more than clear glass;
it's a mirror too,
and we must see how looking back
means seeing through.

Black women and men,
our smooth faces wear old lines.
We cannot see behind the angry eyes
nor curve the stuck out lips
nor stop the helpless hand in mid air
nor quiet the thunder of our blaming
nor open the slammed doors,
shut dreams and closed remembering
till we tuck in our feelings
and step back through the years
with the tilted head of meaning to be free.

Our LOVE ain't EVOL,
but we must return to all the mirrors
that we have been stood up to or laid before,
stand the images on their heads
and lay the reflections to rest forever
that we may stand up inside
and lie together again.

Mirrors,
the spotless grain of the cabin floor,
showing small of back and broad back turned.

Mirrors, mirrors,

spic and span walls and waxed white tile
showing soft bone and empty hard fists at home.

Mirrors,
the streets smoothed by smooth soles
showing rough projections and tender cheeks tough.

Mirrors, mirrors,
the sparkling marble and polished porcelain
showing slumped shoulder smell of outhouse within.

Mirrors,
the scrubbed white skin and tide clean clothes
showing muscles untended and faint flex of coin.

Mirrors,
the clear concrete and washed wood
showing red too bad for blood
and dust too bleak for black.

Mirrors, mirrors,
through the rubbed tears
of quiet woman eyes and loud
and the brass cries of our slack balls and tight sack
shows the spit of the mixed cross
for ungodly years.

We must see it all back
we must see it through
till the evol of our love
is wheeled in the real world
to become at least a kiss we can throw
toward the union of our lips forever.

For Your Questions

Your questions blare
and my shoulders slump again.
I know the origin
but my arms are too short
to raise the beaten slave from dirt sheets
where he stood horizontally.

Nor can I persuade
his living shadows
that squeezing charmin
is not the sole way
to breath above shit
or that the best root
is not fixed
below the belt.

But I have tried to show
my sons the way ahead
by living my love for you
and reminding them that their sisters are women,
and every girl may be mother or sister too.

The boys strutting in old jockey straps
far from the slats of new baby cribs
won't stop preening in millions,
and black daughters will cry awhile yet
as they watch little worlds
lifted on big hard dreams.

I have made the shift inside
to mix the soft and the stiff,
and I carry your eyes with me everywhere
to guard for signs of old cabin floors
and keep our love above dominion.

Black Axe: Cleaving for Song

Next mornings,
we butt butts while stretching,
yawning toward separate edges of dawn.

This is a ritual,
but one we must cut apart
to fit ourselves to song.

Come,
let us go back before last nights,
before our encirclements
to the round locks that mashed us
past flat turning over.

Let us repeat the promise
we whispered in blood and bile,
"we shall never forget,
we shall never forget,"

and then quicken
to the washed out fields
and the washed out faces,
to those warm snows so cold
we winked to keep our eyes open,
"we shall never forget,
we shall never forget"

till we flesh in the last white shadows
where plaster and bleached footpaths
kept out print washable
and our knuckles the color of palms,
pointing no way to noon

where standing is without sides,
"we shall never forget,
we shall never forget."

Come this way with me
cautiously yet free
to where sealed lips probe deeper
than forked tongues,
and limbs never lattice
for positions of double crossing.

Come! I'll come!
We are no enemies
who have to deflect our intimacy
with distance and dialect.

Roll over! I'll roll over!
This is no trick.
I need four arms for contact
and four legs to stand.

I can't go it alone.
I need your curves to make my muscles supple.
I need your womb to rise again
in loving opposites of our same.

I still want to be free.
I have not forgotten
freedom begins in pairs,
and whatsoever I have done
in looking over you while loving you,
I shall seek to mend by looking up.

Next morning,
let us pull the sheets taut together,
leaving them dark with the clean of each other.

Our behinds have no fingers,
and those which mimic our wide mouths
can only cling to air.
Their axe with wedge blade cleaves,
and leaves close hips but separate heads.

I want you near at the inside kiss.

Words

For years I have practiced the sounds
my eyes and ears teamed to learn
when I was young,

and often I have aimed to develop
clear pictures of my mind
in the darkhouse of air
to show my inside face
to the watching thoughts of a woman.

But I have only found sufficient light
for sharp images
when I have screamed
or quietly centered my hate.

Then she saw my likeness,
but it was not worth asking for,
much less carrying around.

At least,
I needed the clicks of sweet noise
to turn out crisp
and be admired,
that I might believe again
space could not be seen
because it was an illusion,
and so distance a production of man.

African woman,
this poem is my portrait;
and if you hold it up to your mind,
you'll glimpse an ancient spirit
smiling at you,
and you will know what I used to be

if you know yourself
and what I want to be again.

And you will understand
that the West does not know itself,
that it is a prodigal child of ours
whom the caves and cold made a killer,
who for its sanity had to deny
the unity of all things
and separate language from the soul.

I will touch you in the wholeness of time,
and having already met
in the silence of this song,
our hands will take our forms,
and we shall speak as parts of each other.

Then I will never doubt
the power of Nommo again.

Beside the Movement

So often,

when my back balks in cheap contoured chair
in the chirping dark of dawn,
and I close the clean black book,
continuing to mark my stare;

or when
my feet speak to straight spine
after walking thee shifts of sleep
through the thick of club law in the streets
to keep awake the dream of freedom;

or when
the gravel of my voice threatens to whisper roll or stop,
and the gravel of my eyes gathers deep in my small,
slipping toward the front seat
during seventh midnight meeting that week;

I need the back of a black woman
to push against,
to sit straight with her against the foe,
enlisting armies from our history;

and want her standing next to me
against avowed and unwitting enemy
to search contrapuntal strength
in mixing of the rhythms of our feet
and two heads above the clouds;

and seek the stripped silk of her speech,
the red wise of clear eyes
to be home with me
when we have helped sharpen talk to being.

So often, afterwards,
just the small of her back in the large of my hands
would straighten forever the bend in me,
point my tottering feet ahead,
and stir the gravel of my voice and eyes

even firm

to love.

Love in Season

Anymore,
when I wonder why
love seemed late
and tapped me from behind,
I remember the nothing of never
and that I could not see
very far in front of me
till you added your eyes.

Then,
there is no need to scold time
for admitting you only
when I was grown enough to be love.

Love is so hard to recognize
when you live black as dark,
and even when you praise the accident,
it keeps you too awake to dream.

And so,
I risk the miss and hit of language
to approach my feelings,
to explain what I can corner on the page.

You are the breath I needed for air,
the mix of bronze and deed
to stir my touch to trembling,
yet keep me searching for midnight dawn.

I love you for all the lives you love,
for the way your center never fades
yet reaches out to brush the pale with hue,
and for sweet dizziness when I stand still.

This was no late encounter,
just the tick of wheel within the wheel,
the fit of freedom and accounting,
the need of half for the round.

God is on time,
good is on time;
the rhyme of seasons is heat and cold,
not the pedometer of days.

Love is
matching the parts to whole,
using the accident of skin,
the count of sun without, within,
to begin forever with two.

How Could I Not Love You?

How could I not love you?

I see you take cracked mirrors from our children,
catch enough sun in your hands to toy their days,
rock them to rising with the love noise in your room,
and lock their knees in place with your praise.

Your straight look was a thick paddle with holes.
They took your tapers to burn their oil
and said their prayers with your syllables.

You wore the halo of their smile.
They carried your name softly in kid titles,
bowing with straight spines and lifted eyes.

Bringing new woes and old wounds,
they watched you refuse to watch the watch,
kissing them with wisdom of happy ever after.

How could I not love you?

Holy

If we had not talked so long at first
about how to change the world,
how much there was to do
and how close serving was to breathing;

if we had not seen the pointed fire
nor felt it blush our cheeks
when evil was the word we rode
upon the air to bridle it;

if all that unbridled passion
had not wet the sheets of feeling
before we floated down to heat
the cool white underneath,

perhaps I would not have expected
our bodies to burst in rhythm.

But we had heaved and panted
so long in love with a world to come,
trembling at the holy touch
of open arms for each other,

I knew when we closed them around ourselves,
our worlds would come together.

Nuptials

You fit in the folds of my arms,
your fingers in the spaces of mine,
but it is not that I define you,
for I sit in the places of your love.

We have assumed positions of survival,
turning top and front to our side;
we are the end of grafted anger,
merging dreams of half a thousand years.

We are another beginning,
a sphinx emerging from fire before ash,
whole from the annealing heat,
head and body of one.

It is Egypt once more;
we shall show answers to save the children.
We are the reasons Africans could wait,
the evidence of their faith.

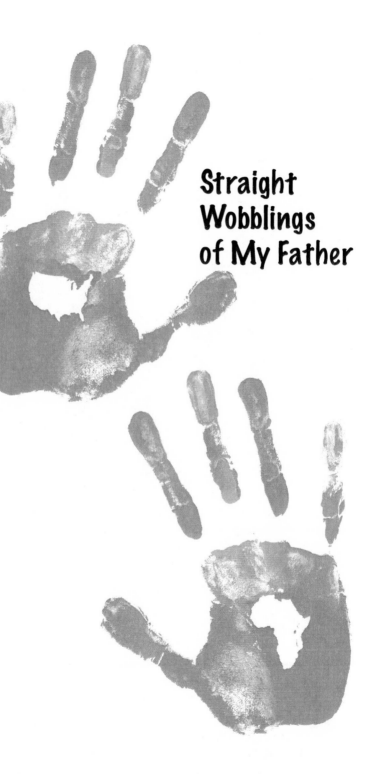

Straight
Wobblings
of My Father

Africa to Me

Africa to me
is a half century of mixed meanings,
cannibal and saint,
ape and genius,
midnight and sun,
victim and warrior never undone.

A boy in a newly integrated school,
I used chalk to whip neat children
in figuring fourth grade blackboards,
but was beaten back by history films
of Africans readying pots for white entrails
and by Tambo and Bones
from nigger heaven
in their neighborhood theater.

Cooked raw so much with learning,
I took colored and Negro as safe ways
to resist the brand of Africa,
and almost lost myself in grand marks
of going across town to their place.

Long before my desk job,
Africa raised the flags of freedom,
and I could not salute them
with hat in hand
or head between my knees;

and so to pay highest respect,
I had to look self straight in the eye
and swear to work
for more than cloth in skies
for Africans everywhere.

Africa to me
is now both pyramid and bone,
claiming much good first, beauty and soul
as well as some blood that's gone.

Africa is my yellow face
loving the race with hands,
understanding we all can claim our place
when we learn its record
and practice the ancestral wish
to be alive for others.

Reading Too Much Music

We have been in this place too long.

Hooked on white melody,
we struggle less
to keep our own rhythm.

We sing daily strange songs in our freedom,
uncommon to old Black folks
in a new land.

We dance death daily,
going our separate ways;
heads full of cold steam,
racing round and round
catching our tails.

Maybe if we knew how
this song and dance began,
those histories would be
more than words to the wise.

It was the new arrangement,
freedom suites for the light
to bear the awful anthems.
Then they found some
forgetting kin, blind within,
numb to all but raw solos.

More of us do now.

Yet others who
are clear about the note of blood
work drums in these cotton fields.

All of us are African.

We must take our music to heart,
be smart enough
to learn death scales
so we will not play them
as fat skeletons
and be buried alive.

Africa on My Mind

Last year I laughed easy
when my tears spread on a page
written to catch black love
and made a perfect Africa.

That glorious blot
mapping the home of my heart,
an intriguing accident then
to tease an hour into smiles.

Then yesterday, bobbling eggs,
I could not keep time of both
and felt wet at my toes,
yellowish splash.

On waxed linoleum tile
frozen in my tracks,
I looked down at a form of Africa
exact as that last year on the page.

I went to bed with this strange happenstance.

Dreams found no words
to fit those frames,
so every poem of mine left the room
minutes before I was to share sound and quiet
of them with crowds
of neighbors from our heart's home,
neither in my hands or head.

In dream I ran, crying everywhere I knew
to find enough of what I meant
to be enough of what I hear and speak.

I awoke without the work of freedom.

Africa is all that is clear.

It is the only form I take
from speech of my fluid beginnings.

Dry Bones of Freedom

More than bone deep,
this freedom to be
the whole world,
to count for everything,
to question what is real
but self
is locking us in cells
tighter than those awful holds,
with only bars for light.

Tomorrow needs a sun
and air that keep us together,
yet there is nothing overhead
but gutless dreams,
and the stench
that cuts black touching fingers
closes us off.

We know the bones,
those still talking stories
in fertile African minds,
those swollen to flesh
with oceans of then and now,
those that summon us to rhythm.

We know how to play those bones.

We know flat sounds of bones too thin to stand,
too dry to keep a beat,
too bleached

to be a black bone
whose freedom is tied to those
who connect and rise

and walk the earth,
assuring
the single freedoms of integration
are kept in separate cells
tomorrow.

Black Time

When it comes my time
to take my time
while the quick take second turns
around my steady gait;

when it comes my time
to pray my time
while the young I've taught scream
and sing martial songs;

I will not bide my time
in warm rocking chairs
or cool porch swings
or sweet memories,

but walk till second crawl
and hum the battle hymn,
loving the feel of spring again,
feeling the love of seasoning.

Hands that cocked the trigger
to protect Africans
will not be twiddling thumbs;
eyes that leveled aim
will be too clear for mere reflection.

Arms that wrestled enemies
will never be fat without sinew;
feet that knew our terrain
will never keep spats clean.

When it comes my time
to mark my time,

my hands will tremble with pointed pens,
soothe backs of those in the field,
make silhouettes on proper walls,
and never stiffness to yield;

my eyes will remain in combat,
slower but sure in war zones,
have time to hold my woman more,
showing soft victories to our own;

my feet will march quietly,
stepping the short way to the heart,
pointing the running the right way,
giving the bounding a start.

Real Malcolm

You, carpenter of solid dreams,
tall as you needed to be
to see life and look death in the eye;
no dunce caps or leashes for you
nor chaining pats on your head
where once had been the lye.

Growing, confessing,
confessing, growing,
professing your love for all
who need a better world
bad enough to burn for it.

To be on fire for human kinship,
to set fire to dead wood of American dreams,
leaning toppling castles of greed,
ash sticks we become when we maim;
to melt the horrible lines
of shade and sunshine
that keep us above, below, outside
each other.

Your X is still the crossroads.

We go where we choose to go.

We go where we know to go.

We go where we have to go.

Your X is still the flashing signal
that warns of unfeeling monsters
who crush bone and spirit in their path,
living leavings

on both sides of their tracks.

Your X is the junction
when we meet to get on board,
and move to the new days,
souls of Africa standing
to work soft stones who stay.

El-Hajj Malik El-Shabazz: Going Through Changes

At eighty-eight,
Malcolm would have sat down with us,
listening to lines of private freedom,
making it plain
that either we keep each other or die.

He would remind us now
how some thought
revolution was songs of overcoming,
a turning of precious cheeks,
a sharing of dollar signs,

and say again
from the main text of his life
that revolutionaries are lyrics of sweat,
are meek when credited with change,
and have no price.

In his strength,
Malcolm would cry at the small size
of our freedom,
our one wish with all candles lit,
the willingness to forget
to be remembered.

He would fall without new firing,
wondering why
his end of hustling
and beginning of passion for women
were yet not enough
for us to understand
community is our largest self.

Remembering Malcolm 48 years after his death

Independence

I do not need to ship you back,
packing you squeeze tight
like white-belly-livered rats
to one of your desolate sites;

I do not need to feel your neck
crack and break at each vertebrae,
charred to bone dust and fleck
past recognition of your ghastly face;

I do not need to split your family
to keep my children wearing gold;
rich is a warm feeling for me
allowing sweet sleep outside your cold.

I do not need to count the cost.

Souls are neither feather nor flesh.

You are past reckoning loss.

I can weigh but fractions of the debt.

I do not need to curse your name
to break the terror of forsaken years.

I do not need your full grave
to make my own life appear.

Invited to the White House

The embossed note was clear:
"Your presence is requested."

In the lovely hand of database,
my name was forged fresh,
with only genuine text
dividing me
from labored push of president.

I caught my breath at
"the company of honored Americans,"
amused to know I need not
defend once more bearded warnings
of this country's death.

I was safe enough now
to be bought into the fold:
clean shaven,
loud curses gone from the last book,
out of closet to lash my own.

I lost my breath again.

Where was that Black legacy
of turning down
dry plums?

When did honored Americans say no
to make the world safe for democracy?

Who found the guts for sacred silence
or at least sent their words alone?

All those images returning
of shaking hands
and stolen embraces,
drinks half gone
and smiles sure lacing

(All shapes, colors, ages, athletes,
politicians, entertainers and others who
thought they reigned in that space)

forced me to seal the card
and search the log
for those without plantations.

Children of Violence

Why is there such blind surprise
about soft hands pulling at steel?

In American field and factory, a child's
fingers have long been bent to feel
sharp hard contours of staying alive.

Massas died in wishful heaps or real
when bolls cut skin far too young
to build thick or lines against quick blood,
or when bleached bone it wrapped around
had lost the smell of meat.

And on clean cabin floors
lay piles and piles of shot white faces
without enough arms to break down doors
to leave awful rapes
or tender eyes cocked for more.

Life has seldom held first place here.

Born and bred in the death of desire,
it is clear alike from broken candles
and golden sties, breath is what you buy.

Guns drip with dollar bills.
Both make baby fat lean
before they kill.

Why is there such blind surprise
about soft hands pulling at steel?

Black Judgments

Those of us who understand
the carnage of Black women and men
have to go further now
while we tend the victims,
clearing the battlefields.

We must build and make judgments again
in our best tradition.

We who remember
must change the story
that is told for us,
that we will forever be
against each other.

"My own thing" is killing us;
We are each other's business.

We must enlarge the frame of images
for those old only as their breathing
and find the will to triumph.

If we continue to turn
away from each other,
it will not matter
that we were burnt offerings.

Our children will not be
or they will not be our own.

Inspired by words from Gwendolyn Brooks

No More Centuries

It may take another hundred years
before more souls of Black folk
have memory or heart enough
to resist sucking white holes of success.

We do not have that time.

We are more our own enemies now,
foes of colored in the everywhere South.

We must go down with the dispossessed
and not the kidnappers of this globe.

It is too late to blame such thieves
for our wishing the American dream
and being blind to those from whom we steal.

We who know or feel ourselves
must show young the ends of that desire.

We must love them to memory and heart
and build a pyre for all the rest.

No One

It is new year's old match again,
masters contending to be the one;
black backs now pass and run
rainbow teams to zones that end.

The rose bowl—
walls rising till they bend
and shape a world that sends
gladiators to their goal,

while many warm inside
join this sport between the lines,
forgetting galaxies of dark souls
who run for cover from bitter cold.

And we, the in crowd,
packed spoonlike in snow and sun
repeat signs of life with white tongues,
black fingers pointing out loud.

We are number one.
We are no one.

We remember marks well enough
to throw the game.

We can be quarter of a back,
can be body with part brain,
can be president some day
and help the country sack
the rest of nether neverlands.

Those few in front offices call
the play and get the fall,
and we forget for what we stand.

Dropping Names and Soul

Before the next census comes,
and some of us break records
to change our race,
let us check the awful cost
of what would be spirited away.

The records say we are Africans
who did not choose this cold and white,
but came resisting, splitting chains
with the sharp heat of desire
to never lose ourselves.

The cost of this colorless kidnapping
was broken hymens, necks and dreams,
yet some seem quite willing now
to cross over this time,
too lost in that thieving, lying world.

We are more than African words.

We are the strength of living links
to the way of life that is community,
or we will enter the next thousand years
counting only as other.

Mixing Black Metaphors

So many answers have been given
to our wherefores in this place;
we were stolen to heal the thieves,
we were stolen to find ourselves,
we were stolen because men steal.

Some the less,
we are here,
without the welcome light,
without wages for building empire,
without credit or even gratitude

and

we are here in the paunch of the whale,
Jonahs with fresh blubber jones,
making fat we do not own,
living for the day of yawning.

Sometimes,
it seems all accounts would be settled
by removing Africa from our name
for a better reason than we shunned it;

to cut the hide apart,
and let the hind quarters of our lives
walk headless across the land
without defiling black origins.

So all of us here who choose
could roll with wide mouths in feces,
integrating limbs and laughter
to be dark undersides
of the plunderers of colored worlds.

But then
I notice natal sons of the motherland
who lattice legacies and lust
with pale progeny who parent now,

so I realize first the point of our being here
is to heal the thieves
while annealing ourselves,

and finally that
we must tract enough memory
to understand the highwayman
in our children.

America to Me

America to me
is a weak animal
stumbling around with white sheets
over its small head
and black gauze underneath belly
having dragged awful ground
too long ever to be clean.

A pale strong wolf once
because it ran in thick packs,
it stood always on hind legs
to attack and devour all of us
coaxed or forced from home
or caught unawares alone.

I forgive the tearing of limbs,
disfiguration of flesh,
even bloated guts and slack faces,
even the picked dry bones,
for skeletons are not fresh history.

But never, never can America atone
for mutilations within my people,
the desire to be a dark wolf
and yet be bleached,
those inner hungers so hard
to keep from the door.

America to me
is a weak animal now,

wild-eyed at entrapment in the deep pile
of some mended souls,
threading our broken spirits and bones,
dangerous to death with old desires
and growing fears
of African encirclements.

The Rhythm of Home

If I could show you a time before
when death sat in for life,
when such a swap was he,
we trusted him to stand.

If I could lead you back to spaces
we walked waking with bound hands,
you would come to us again.

But Africa is farther than years or stretch.

Private pulses cannot keep being.

Yet, in this land where one is prime,
we selected others for breathing,
renewing a way to cut silences
to close as polyrhythm in our heads.

To a Black Father After Fifty

When you were only fifty,
candles left too much smoke
for your fire to run through,
and Mom's sweet but heavy cake
clogged more than clear arteries.

Fifty is a memory for us both now,
and I wonder what more
than an extra breath is required
to be granted the aching wish
for deep years with dark glow?

I do not know.

I am beginning to understand
how birthdays leave crumbs with smiles,
celebrations with tallow in the bowl
never to be with wick again,
that strength and weak are all man.

So with you, I seek to cull
rich stuff to fatten the light left
in our shorter but firmer stakes,
to teach those watching in bare rooms
to work a wish of life too full

to snuff in any single blow.

Strong Enough to Need You

It is with you
I mount the courage
to travel the dense past,
that thicket of thin brushings.

It is with you
I find uncracked mirrors
to piece ugly silvers
into a picture I like again.

You, getting me straight,
loving me to narrows
I needed but did not know,
holding my confusion in.

You, making me pretty,
touching up features I hid
from the world and myself,
teaching all health is within.

There is only my life left
to thank you
for loving away the scars.

Straight Wobblings of My Father

He taught me how to walk without wobbling.

Watching unsure steps,
he would steady me with eye and measured distance,
hands close enough to catch.

And,
between my trials,
he walked the chalk of Black manhood,
leaving unsmudged blue lines
of how to stand
then look ahead to find the balance,
knowing he was behind.

Last week,
I took him out to try new house shoes,
watching his silent count
of steps to the first fitting chair,
and I lost my grip
even with both hands prepared
to hold him up.

His getting places
seemed so out of my hands,
I marveled again
how easy he made my ancient trip
from crawl to open arms.

Once the slippers were found
deep enough to hold swollen ankles,
I ached again for his early wisdom
of quiet assurance
that hands were there
if I would trust my legs and him.

Sunday Bootleg Saviors

All of them now are gone.

Saturday's long distance sound
in the bright middle of day
was not a warm how have you been
from my old hometown
but a report from a sober friend
that the last of Sunday saviors
had slipped away
to some world without weekends.

I had not needed them for a while.

My smile had turned up
before the first death,
but I would not have the breath
to tell this story
if any one of them
had shut his door

when I roped veins,
begging alcohol I could not pay for
to keep down my swelling head
the day bars were closed,
and I could not shake
enough precious drops
from the bottles I would mate.

Soaked steadiness then
locked quiet legs into place,
and I could face
the loud stupor of a death wish
until seven Monday morning.

Sunday saviors
pulled me through dry church bells
and barred gates to hell
until I tired of shut eyes
and liquid laughter
from mouths
I did not recognize.

Hothouse Flowers: Speaking with Inmates

You are there
after the unbroken fall.
No grass in your cell,
pillow hard if at all.

Standing up, muscles bulge.
You walk to used instruments of song,
fingering tight strings and, through slight holes,
push sweet music along.

You had summoned me to your set.
Rebuilding African American men,
you called me to confinement
to break out inside before the sun again.

The anthem, the universal prayer,
your moving in this vertical hold,
resisting more narrow horizons
is sacred service of your fold.

I start talking to ourselves,
reading renewal of young Black males,
the print of quiet rising speech to each other
mocking the flat page, loving the braille.

I keep turning as I walk with you,
reflecting the best in your eyes and brow;
dark heat warms and thaws deep ice,
and from the furrows' water, flowers grow.

We are there.
Our love is sure ledge.
More cracked flowers push through concrete.
New cracks lead back to our street.

Respite

Fall is a lump in my throat,
misty eyes
while a smile wide to its edges;

sun filled trees
mothering miraculous children,
rainbow loves of the next world.

All October,
I do not play the car cassette.

My ears absorb
what my eyes cannot hold.
The knot is too large
to praise music.

Fall colors insist
that I rest from the countryside
of black and white
till I get home,

that I forget
the short and long winters.

Black Boy Needing a Brother

I remember horrible waits
to find a shadow
at some right time of day,

and though advised so many times
where and when I stand,
I ended up alone
in different spots steps away
from a new brother's hands
to play ball with.

Having been taught
the need for doubles
was a pale desire
for those too weak
to hear another voice speak,

I promised to stand aside
or even be covered
by a little brother
if he would just arrive
and stay in sun with me
for the life of pitch and catch.

You came after solitudes
of annual all-star games
I staged in the unwatching backyard
that Negro leagues always won,

the first of us
in a white hospital room
without dust of home,
and when you smelled enough clean air
to be delivered with Mom

to our covered world,
I stood on the washed wooden porch
with my first mitt,
took the small cap off,
saluting you,

softly touching your new hands,
willing to wait
even as I planned
to work your fingers into big bone
until my glove would fit.

Some say we look alike now,
but not because either stands
in the shadow of the other.

Your hands have helped so much.

Jackie moved to their majors
the year after your birth,

but you have loved leagues into play
I never dreamed of
when I was a lonely boy
seeking proper places to stand,
wanting only to be joined.

Taking Whippings for Each Other

There is wisdom in tears
if they slide away
from human centers
or if they dry and
lend cheeks character to set.

Our eyes wet at whimperings
of brothers and sisters
who braved deathlike swats
of rolled tight newsprint,
rulers too big for measuring,
and switches snatched low
from signifying trees,

we asked
why not share the tears
to leaven laughing?

Our world was one block,
and we looked enough alike
to play out the differences.

We soft kids
who kept our right
to lead against playmates' pains
yet took blood
while fighting with all left
to win the most trophy heads.

Two rules
for taking each other's whippings
were that the saved

not bring planned pain into lives

who would trade innocence
for clenched eyes,
or ever be weak enough again
to repeat that violation.

This was the tradition then
in the predictable world of colored dolls and peddle cars,
wagons, skates, and tricycles,
homemade teeter-totters, swings,
doll houses and all other things
we saw moved to be by love.

This is our tradition now,

home of a family never divided.

Let us take each other's whippings
as long as no one
devises pain as a way to live
or is not so weak
that flopping to past mistakes
stays sweet.

Saluting Kin Who Are Black and Poor

Life is breath,

death is breathless,

but they have always been
and gone together.

Kin is life,
and is death only when
those crossed by blood
are thinned
by the water of things
or not remembering.

Saluting loved ones
is never straight armed
or planned flick of air;
it is the bending hand
that remains there.

Black relations
beat back before deep waters
were damned
to drown our blood
or at least thin
the memory of Africa.

And though casualties keep mounting
without wide rich eyes fixed
for days to honor the goings,

we hail long lines of simple spirits
whose hard gentle hands
stretched out to yield,
to work the thickness
of claiming even one drop
as next of kin.

Bronze Plated Mother

Reaching your mother's years,
sputtering to the next room
head down at your shortest height,
teaching even yet to smile at fears,
marching ahead erect
even when the floor comes up to meet you.

Brown spindly girl
in the stout of a sister's heart,
father's cheers and mother's quiet support;
finding legs under you
more than your own,
you stepped up to do whole worlds proud.

Bronze plated girl
first in your class,
going gold with motherhood,
you taught me how to toe big boy lines,
but how being boy was not enough.

We were born of girls
you showed,
and if they moved as free,
I would be strong.

Gladly,
I have never loved a weak woman.
I have always looked for what you are,
and, no doubt, because of you,
I have often been struck by brown girls.

In the somehow mix of you and Dad
and both your parents,
my face missed the gorgeous brown,

and that may be why
I vaunt my high forehead
and wide nose
as well as all other visible signs
of being African.

I come up short.

But you have taught
the heart of Africa,
the lovely deep dark
of living for the beat of community.

I would like to borrow your faith
for the rest of my life
and a piece of the word
that lets you smile
when you return to bed or chair
and your face lifts
from the uncomplained walk
between the ends of the house,
your body's limits of the world.

Know Children Here

If there are no children here,
the sun has already gone out,
and when the heavy sky drops down,
there will be no large star close enough
to give us light.

They drop in first grade, tired
of too little and too much,
hoping for miracles in a book
to make the point and renew surprise,

but
the exercise is finding the match
of school and home.

There is no account of thin and thick
they feel is surely deserved.

There is only the mature plight.

The poor and rich both know
of bad heads posing love for gain,
of danger and death in family,
how a starved child has no chance to cry,
much less to be.

Our children are fresh rivers in an old world
from which new civilizations grow,
or they are our last cesspools
killing as their own lives run dry.

Swishing Pants and Pitching Caps

The small two-room stucco school
where new corduroy pants swished first
and my cap landed good days
on the second row of hooks
was also the citadel
of kids with a single skin.

In that geography of no North
where my aunt led me to Booker T.,
red, white, and blue democracy was
raised and lowered each day outside
while level loving looks stayed within.

All of us Negro children grinned
when we saw such large selves in her eyes;
young colored woman from Delaware
gone west to Indiana to live her faith
that souls of black folks would not die.

Some called it segregation;
busing had nothing to do with time,
second-hand readers turned to classics,
hope was another nursery rhyme.

The half gong of a century moves to sound,
and I with pants to keep air quiet,
with fancy cap of some alma mater,
was hooked to believe things have changed
or even remained the same.

In Illinois, a same state,
I look now at young in front, around,
seeing every horizontal way, I find
my faith in them to be bigger than me
and to lift all souls who seem to die.
But I am not as wise as Ms. Starks.

To these kids the world is new, at
least velvet; they fly with drops of hat.
History is too old a fact.
There is no blood on their hands.

They are nice guys, with appointed wives,
or girls who dream to be like men.
The O.J. trial was the first lynching,
a million men marched against women and whites;
right affirmative action exposes the idle.

I cannot get them to circle the past.
Pleasantly they mark the answers for tomorrow.
When I catch a knowing glance, they drop eyes
and talk lightly after class.

Maybe they are right.

I am too far away from the two-room school
or too close to the ivy green here
to know which questions mean,
much less to lead to swish answers
or practice of pitching the right cap.

Jumping the Broom and Crossing Sticks

Yesterday,
in our watched weddings,
we jumped the broom
to start our run in life together.

We crossed the right sticks
so stones who may break bones
would never hurt us with words
and never, never name.

Black love moves were never limbo,
though we have bent in incredible ways
to keep ourselves free from games
of those who were their only miracles.

Black home making is sweeping together,
sweeping away past debris,
sweeping up piles of times so high
you sweep each other off your feet forever.

Black Woman Keeping Me Young

Before your smile,
I rose each morning
slipping to cracked mirrors,
fully expecting to see
furrowed brow or squinting eye
when I did not recognize me.

I did not count on sudden gray,
new hanging jowl,
lines gouged by one hard sleep
in this ceremony of looking for old
but just a picture changed enough
to stop the razor for a thinking pause.

My children claimed as rule
Black folks did not show age
and I had good genes beside,
that laughing had kept skin tight
and I worried none about finishing schools.

But I thought
their fingers in my eye
left age a blur
or my looking out for those
who had been taught
dark must run from mirrors
or be cracked white enough
to want to be recognized.

But since I have wakened
with your smile,
I need not leave our bed to rise
and see my unbroken face
or stand with you
to be a good reflection.

Quilting Races Together

When we watch hands at work,
the timeless stitch of difference
whose regular rhythm is love,
we see patches seamed to whole.

Soft threads allow some early space,
short pull of skeptical pieces
too large or little on their own,
angling to save that special face;

yet also hold the human tie
in cold sweat of turbulent sleep,
in the brittleness of hot ice,
in the scalding of history's fire.

We are lovely strips without run
who would rather give warmth than hang.
We know the richness of our cover,
the cheapness of a smear of one.

We are handiwork of things to be.
Stretched, frayed, our colors stay.
We are the pattern for tomorrow;
quiet quilts are human destiny.

It Is Where My Heart Was Born

It is where my heart was born
and where I must return;
centuries are secondhand ticks
I have fixed with memory
to be in the same sun of Africa,

and the missing city signs
of my first hue and cry
mean only my home is larger,
a continental black space
to claim and hold high.

My yellow on edges skin deep,
I live to be part of the great spot,
the density of soul that will spread
until community is once again
the lot we all have cast.

Africa to me is right rhythm,
now lonely stuff of black wholes.

We are touch with time to listen
though more particles spin past gravity
into the smallest world of one.

I have been taught seven millennia
that community is both natal cord
and tied wonderfully to forever,
so I try to be at one
with the little circle that is left.

And slow I reach for hands of those
who cut their fingers to bleed my own,
whose knuckles smashed my skin,
who counted ways to keep me
working free with gunpoint smile;

for the soul of Africa is such size
I cannot hold tomorrow against infirm
or frighten the blameless child.

Into Africa,
Being Black

The Rivers Speak of Negroes

We've seen negroes,
ancient and living negroes
who hate dusk
and rise only with dawn;
our souls have not emptied like negroes.

We saw them in classical Egypt
struggling against Nubians and themselves;

we saw them in glorious Spain
believing civilization was a dark age,
unwilling to stand with Hannibal,
or be Moor.

The Nile flowed west
through the Mediterranean and Atlantic,
filling the Ohio and Mississippi
with living black carcasses,
making beds too hard to sleep in.

We saw them at the Taras
reminding masters they were house slaves,
strangers to African flesh
and soil in the fields,
whose soft hands carried red designs
to their gods,
setting fire to just rebellions.

We saw them passing out
when standing up
meant too large a target
for sacrifice.

We see them thinking massa now,
owning lean plantations
for small prices of smaller souls,
wanting to be only teeth
that show up in the night.

We've seen negroes
ancient and living negroes
who hate dusk
and rise only with dawn;
our souls have not emptied like negroes.

Waiting for God(ot) to Come Down

Swinging on a washed wooden porch
was joy for generations of the race,
though scrubbed children would wait
so Black adults could be lifted up.

Sundown time was for tired workers
in the house or from the mill to sit,
room for elders' comfortable fit;
easy rocking squeaks filled smiles
as god appeared in the evening.

This was not a sundown town
where dark skin was restless at night.

Something in that first swing low
was above our young heads;
the porch made more noise than us,
though we never heard it.

Next day, children tried to recreate
the ritual that brought out stars and moon
but could only laugh at small lifts,
wondering why our short legs
honored no commands to let us down
so we could dream of the sacred seat.

Today,
swings speak another way.

Across the street,
a White man in his nineties and wife
wait sweet days
and nights together

where weather permits
for something I do not yet see.
I seldom hear them talk,
see them face each other in their quiet;
tough shoulders stay in touch
and hands must speak.

They may have been loud at lynching flings
where Blacks were set rocking in trees,
when my parents and theirs
retired from their light heavy world
to find tomorrow's promises in swings,

but now feeling their silence,
I try to understand where life is heading,
whether jerking heads that scream
rock in the same world
as old privileged faces remembering
something.

Nothing is clear
but fertile memories of our old porch swing
and that I find little joy
in the solemn waiting I cannot hear.

Beyond Vietnam

It is more than Glen Beck
having a different dream at the Memorial,
claiming it the same as yours;

it is more than the right changing contexts
of your hope we all be measured
by the content of our character;

it is more than funds being less sufficient
than then to cash in well earned checks;
empty hands are now the ones to blame.

Wilderness has always been inside,
and it keeps growing
in the face of pretty ads for gold;
we seek barren promised lands
that you warned about
and never would have gone to with us.

We have more money in fewer pockets,
holding sacred rituals to justify
the hungry, homeless and jobless
who do not try hard enough;
fat bonuses return in a half blink
while others starve or
drop head between thighs to live.

Your last nightmares were larger than race,
so you went to Memphis,
a great ancient Black place,
to center the picture of wealth and want,

and would have lived in shantytowns
at marble edges of the Capitol,

but more than one planned to make sure
you quit looking over mountaintops
to point out promised lands for all.

Some of us are tired of broken toys
and of others broken by them,
fear our own emptiness
and glut that will not let us rest,

and the young across color lines
in college discussion rooms
are sitting up while growing up,
taking notice of hidden worlds
they pass by.

We may not get to mountaintops with you.

We cannot look over and see the promise
until we stand on early shoulders,
feel the heartbeat of their place,
and work beyond poverty, war, and race,

beyond Vietnam.

A tribute to Dr. Martin Luther King Jr.

Grid Irons and Spring: To a Best Friend

You waited for spring to die.

New sap from below,
young green shoots on the bow
and a clear day you earned with blood
for all to see forever.

No winter snow for the next bed,
no bare black limbs for sky;
you chose to pass in the fertile laugh
at the promise of life kept alive.

You called me last to this old home
with my parents down the room,
and explained with sure eyes
better than words ever spoken
you were on the sacred goal line
and to keep arms open
to catch the bounce of your best spike.

We had been a Black team,
you patiently storming the line,
I tentatively calling signals
from winning practices.

So you waited for me to travel winters
to see you whole again,
to ease my pain that had cut short chalk sessions,
to put aside my childish need
to always find you
in sacred helmet and pads
with another first and ten.

Your last quiet look insisted

I remember being horizontal,
learning some things are only noticed
from the angle of the earth.

Men get too tall to see pain,
forget to kneel,
and bumping clouds beings lemon rain.

The late stubbing of your toe,
sugar that took it and other precious parts
was life cutting you up to size.
You were wise and well enough to laugh,
deeper than the belly noise we shared
dancing through the smoky nights
in love with suns of summer in our bones.

You have lain on your back for years
and taught tall was just an idea,
that one could stand up from any position.

Slowly, slowly,
I have learned
it is you who has been teacher
in serious plays for freedom,
in grid irons of spring.

Camp Ground Meeting

(For Felix Boeteng)

I should have known
our long last conversation was good-bye;
the phone stayed wet on my ear
and I could not clear the eyes.

You never spent much time
in talking about self;
you worried about worlds looking like us,
yet managed haunting smiles
for ancestors of those who broke us up,
branding us hot with new cold,
dark flesh chattel in fields of white.

That Sunday afternoon,
you chose me as brother
without the hyphens of America
to share the questions
your body was asking.

You said
my faith in good people
and miracles of soil
to heal the sores of bone
was why your trusted me
with secrets of going home
to see a woman of earth,
sink your roots
and become whole again.

You aimed to come back here
to white pills and sterile sick factories
when the spirit was prepared.

You had trusted me with so much before

as we worked to build homes
back in the sun
for all who wanted souls to ripen,
no matter their youth on the earth
or pallor being human.

I trust you now
to steer your free ship ahead
with quiet sure hands
to meet the ancestors.

Fixing Things

You were as good with coarse tissues
as with hammer and saw.

Fixing things,
getting me to get it right,
and swabbing my eyes
so there would be no waste of tears
if my best could not determine the fight.

Even other boys knew
to give it to God
if you came up short.

Nobody else's dad
wheeled a bicycle well enough
to fix children's swings in stone,
make teeter totters with solid framing wood
and mount bells on tricycles
that rain would not rust.

They watched you add sons
without simple siring,
and so put your face
in private places as father.

Now,
I watch you in the two-bed room
working extra shifts of sleep
with no more fuss than young overtime,
and trying to swell lean cheeks
in the nursing home
to keep sweet flesh on thinning bones.

Even in the awfully named retreat,

you come young to me at night
with tight face and straight legs,
breaking my dreams with laughter
that love will always mock age.

You fix yet early thoughts
of curving my spine,
slipping the lock from knees
or wanting seasons of wet breath.

I cannot fix Alzheimer's,
but you are as good as ever
with handless examples in my dreams.

Returning Home

When we were young
and worried about hair going home,
we would run from rain,
hiding after bouts with basin bowls.

As Africans, we should have known
everything loved needs to return.

Yesterday, my brother's wife
curled herself to re-enter the womb,
slipping back unafraid to join
the host, and prepare to welcome
those of us ready to head home.

Because we saw her live black lore
of scared forms with no skin between,
felt her inside in best and worst times,
we count her here and follow the lead
under no less watchful eye.

Yet, we miss the human smile,
the voice pitched with gentle hands,
the stride of flesh and its commands
of straight ahead into the wind.

The spaces she filled have no end.
We are talking in her spirit now.

Mimicking soft unforgettable words,
practicing in pain examples she chose,
remembering her in front, sharing her bow,
we run with tears to clear the way
to keep her proud, to preserve her day.
Everything loved will return.

Father Away

Although I stop so many times
each day to court your smile,
it is at night you come bodily
and live behind closed eyes.

Before dawn this day
after rising to search stubborn sleep
in a book's printed places,
I found heavy lids
and lay down again
to wait for morning.

You rose before sun,
driving first time since Shoneys
some years ago
when we bought Mom's table fun.

Younger than me outside the dream,
you pulled up steady to parsonage door
to carry me once more to light.

Fifteen months now,
you have made plain
tears are not for your going;
night beings a rich relief
for your full and robust shape.

You insist on teaching me
from a wide open grave
that love does not stop with breathing,
death can only seal eyes,
sleep is always sweet forgetfulness
if there is little in daylight to hide.

Dad,
you won't let me miss you.

I tried to be father when you were frail
to save bone parts of your spine,
to keep fevered mouth cool enough to smile,
clear all the while I was son.

Never stop watching my wobbly step,
steady me more with inside secrets
of near worlds mixing,
that flesh is never needed
to keep love we have.

One Fork

Dad quipped so often
about his father and the one fork.

As the last child,
he told his first one,
named after his father,
how he remembered
the sink full of dirty silver,
and one fork was pulled,
washed and used
until his mother came home.

Dad never mentioned plates,
much less a knife and spoon,
and I must guess
there was just one of those too
cleaned up, baptized each time
there was a lonely meal.

But the fork,
with its special sound and place,
became a way to think about turning
more than tuning
and picking up things
when you did not have to cut them
or hold them safely
when they were too thin or soupy
to stab.

My grandfather may have kept the ritual
to remind himself he was alone,
incomplete without his wife,

that keeping all dishes clean
when the love of his life
was not at home
would seem like satiety
disguising emptiness.

It may also have been
his choosing a fork
would remind
no meal was complete without her.

It is silly now I even thought
Dad's story was about
not wanting to wash the dishes.

When his father could not choose
to keep my grandmother
free of hazards of work
for Negro women,
even at one corner of the table
there were smaller reminders
he could not keep her there
if all in front of him
was one fork and warmed over meals.

Another First Decade

In living memory,
we return to their civil war
with one grandfather coming into a world
on the edge of two confederate state stars.

As children,
we heard Guthrie as Mom's ancestry;
no one revealed the map place
looked both Kentucky and Tennessee.

On Dad's side,
slavery seemed finished before parents' start
in North Carolina
but they tried freedom in Indiana,
a state the Klan ran between sheets,
where grandfather closed an opened hand
to their five grand offer in the Twenties
to sell his name to support their man.

For those four bearers,
lives stretched from physical chains
to the predictable death of reconstruction.
Just sixteen years
from oldest to youngest grandparents,
from iron bands on hands and feet
to braided rope leaving necks no hair.

We were from another war and peace.
Roosevelt and Lincoln schools
seemed promising as colored Washington ones,
and mom blew kisses at night
to assure my father, barred from unions,
their children would get it right.

Together, they made a future point
sent neatly to a two-room school
that some *Brown* decision would be a low rule.

Growing up in less than civil rights,
we yet became high like them
when new paper creeds were signed
and old laws crossed through.

That high of integration was too much
for those who thought they would not see it
and others who only saw an early heaven
where dirt from souls would be scrubbed clean white.

Being able to match black with white
was done with closed or squinted eyes
and, with feet unclearly off the ground,
we stumbled to earth in awful surprise.

Even then, we made ways to keep so low,
we would blame those refusing to rise
or soar so high and not be found.

Eulogy for Baby B(r)othering

Called to your rocking chair this time,

it was not easy cradling
of half a century ago when
I was big brother force with fingers
to push your baby body to smile;

this was a cradle with broken arms
that jerked your head up and down,
keeping alive ragged breathing rhythms
with pulse no more than missing sound.

You were the baby of five,
but crown jewel of our parents' past;
you saw your shine as tarnish,
gold that did not want brown to last.

But you were much we were not;

rich copper face of three grandparents,
taller than them and Dad,
our quickest feet on some surfaces,
a body two brothers wished we had.

Perhaps, we knew winding streets better,
ones the rest feared to go,
but did not share their painful memories
of no safety close to home,

but you were made up of even finer stuff
than stories you could make up.

Our father worshipped his brown father,
and lifted closed windows to snatch me,

oldest boy named after his dad,
from turning yellow face to permanent pee.

You found new speeds when ahead,
but did not see over enough with height
to catch shorter, treacherous enemies
who had few wishes to be right.

I thought the ventilator would be mine first
and you would steady my flight.
Why b(r)other?
I lost a brother in towers that bothered.

You saw me on shaking knees.

I wanted to be a painful lesson
of getting up when down was all that seemed,
but was never smart enough
to keep you close enough
to believe my love.

Laurel and Toussaint

Some knew you two would bring
accolades and revolution to the world,
separately for a long short while
and then jointly forever.

Laurel's gift was of the spirit;
her smile ironed out deep wrinkles,
her laugh shamed sorry frowns,
and giving became breath she found.

Toussaint routed short rulers,
bringing freedom to people who got ready,
strong enough to wield sharp swords
from a sheath of soft words.

As children, we were advised
Sunday service was the best place
to find a better half and more
than batting eyes, souls lost in flesh.

We knew the Black church had run
sweet chariots above and underground,
teaching one must be a fugitive
from chains of self and self-hate.

You two were a great campground meeting,
finding love and life can begin at forty,
knowing future is a time that lasts,
for love keeps you young.

Though this poem could never speak
of rhyme and rhythm of your passion
or how you can teach Black doubters
that love does make a way,

let it help you to remember
love knows more than the shadow,
and life is always ahead
so long as you are behind each other.

A Song You Have the Music To
(For Gwendolyn Brooks)

I lifted this song with your books,
read them all again,
shared your love
of saying your love
while you lived it even better.

I looked for your alliterate lovelies
that were too pleased to stand alone,
soft black bridal gowns
lacing the one best dark suit.

But I could not wed them as wisely
as your joining,
nor alter new pairs
for lasting ceremony.

And so I returned to the Howard chapel
that you filled with musical prayer
to offer broken rhythms to the sure cadences
of your life and lyric.

Each day I teach Lincoln in the West
and chocolate Mabbie dreaming marble.
Lincoln wants to be president
and Mabbie sits on her hair in front yards.

We need you here at Howard.
We need the mirrors of your love lessons,
the clean polished glass of your mothering
to show our lives free alliteration.

We need the miracle of your metamorphosis,
the golden choice to pat your fleece,
to jet the double fleecers of your day,
giving us starred night in which to believe.
Broadside was better for your ballista,
and Third World the best way for developing
rich land we thought was arid
just with the power of your singing.

Sing on, Miss Brooks,
with your spring spirit greening us.
Marry us with your wisdom,
with the music of your trust.

I sang with you once, Miss Brooks,
on the banks of a Wabash you made black,
with Haki, a tall son sunning us,
we three lyricing wind at the students' back.

This song is a memorial to a Topeka girl
whose decisions were both black and supreme.
In the forever that is left of your life,
keep us awake with your sonorous dreams.

Ella Baker: Lifted by Others Climbing

When you were eighty and in New York,
too weak to fly to western Maryland
and testify
at a conference on Black women writers
I had been asked to organize,

you transformed my greeting over the wire
into a thirty-minute seminar
on how success seeks you
when the back is turned to limelight.

You spent fifty years leading from back seats of male buses
or at the side of others with no fanfare,
helping them see strengths already there.

Beginning with the times you crossed lines
at a Negro college in the twenties,
widening boundaries for girls under lock and key,
to fighting ministers from on high,

you lived your mantra:
strong people do not need strong leaders.

Young college students, Black and White,
you brought to Shaw when I was a boy
to show listening
is the first act of revolution,
but also has a price
if it is to men
not bashful about claiming right.

Always,
they listened to you;
men followed without losing deep voice,

singing your praise
and calling you blessed when you left this phase.

When listening to you still,
we are lifted by others climbing.

Valleys in Mountaintops

If King were breathing in this phase,
he would not need mountaintops today
to watch our happy wilderness wanderings
more than forty years since Memphis.

We found and lost move so in style,
turn platinum to an awful right,
and come in all colors and genders now
seeking modern action blocks at night
to sell others and ourselves without notice.

King did not live long enough
to see swelling armies march backward
to American dreams of more empty stuff,
with some Black soldiers shooting to lie in front
or least hold up the crumbling rear.

He would warn newest mercenaries
their belly commitment to one per cent
puts them in the eye of final storms,
more deadly than hunger, segregation or chain
that will send them flat under knees
where even prayers cannot be sent.

But King would also say these casualties
come at the same time
young, black, brown, and white together
can move ahead to a promised land
where the covenant is to stand and share.

Remembering valleys in mountaintops,
greedy glacial sculptings,
he would urge us not to wait
until history sores are healed

before we join to live tough dreams
of a future too large to be for one.

The young can move centuries of color and gender lines
to a culture of community
where we are no longer occupied
by the small goblins of self.

With you, we are better than deepening valleys
that took his wind after the dream,
and we can get to what we need
if we resist them when we crawl,
take straight legs and our shoulders
to find fresh air in mountaintops
where all can breathe free.

King: A Class Act

So weary of baubles as a child,
largest allowance in town
noiseless when it fell,
shiny bicycle that hurt the eyes
like looking at sun in middle of mirrors,
and empty exclusive trips the family took
to places King was afraid
to swell cheeks about,

he jumped out windows of home
to land feet on solid ground.

King fought big money in the big house
and proper polished sounds of respectable Negroes
wearing sick smiles in sick lapels.

Scolding posturing peers at Morehouse,
capstone school finishing colored boys,
he found a mentor with guts enough
to laugh in the face of tenure
and teach Negroes classed off too,
a lesson living would not let him forget.

King watched the talented tenth
with tassels on their right
slap black skin off busses in Montgomery
and Selma, marching tight
till power brokers held palms up,
inviting them to sell their own.

King's churches were not blown up,
but sometimes imploded from model members vying
to be head Negro in charge.

The mix of ambitious Blacks
and Whites in charge was too much,

so,
one year before
King was scoped by many eyes,
he preached America needed a revolution of values
at the same church
that had fielded cries of reparation.

Most of us do not see that yet.
going broke loving bad money and other bad bets.

King's last dreams before the mountaintop
were to build shantytowns in front of monuments
near the place some thought us free at last,
and build up garbage workers inside
in the namesake of Black ancient Memphis.

Today, King may have been eighty-four
if he had stopped at civil rights,
if he had heeded crowds to stop at race,
but he had seen there was more
in his family, among friends,
and other leaders on the silver screen.

Growing old was less important
than being a Black class act.

Conversation Dreams of a King and President

Mr. President,
your victory is so sweet
for those who believed the enslaved
would get last laugh at chains,
but this is not yet the promise land
I looked over and saw in Memphis.

Earlier,
I nightmared in Riverside Church
about our violent country
on the wrong side of most revolutions,
where green was a monied way of death
and not an environment of life.

You and other dreamers
have worked aware
in forty wilderness years between.

You were only two
when I shared my dream before Lincoln,
and in the second grade
when they tried to make it mimicry.

Your two girls were born late
to be in that Sixteenth Street church
where flesh and faith were mixed smithereens,
and the next year
young Blacks and Whites like you
were driven to or from their knees
when Boards walked in Atlantic City,
delaying the great freedom party
that was tired of turning cheeks.

Symbolic convention seats meant nothing.
Dreamers from the Mississippi Freedom Democratic party
had not bussed to be just seen.

Our dream allowed you to reach.

Boy and auntie now
will bring thinning crowds,
and Black children without desire
to be anybody's president
will be more at home inside

but the colors of power remain.

You and Michelle
did not need Harvard to know
true colors of this White House.
Through all must believe
it is a reasonable residential stop,
the great greed it rooms
must be brought to light.

Those who now believe in you,
most without means to be the live audience
and increase levels of applause
when you became first Black President,
will tie their future to you
and your transformation dream.

Dr. King,
I have learned meanings of your dream
through courage and sacrifice in deed;
you and my mother refused to flinch
from the broad daylight incubus,
and demonstrated this country's creed.

Africa and Europe met often before,
but stories were told by one
of classic and dark continents;
rape was both charge and reality
for children of the sun.

You were African beyond speech,
color and history;
you practiced the culture of community,
and all were beloved
who were not their own boundaries.

You taught me community organizing
was a larger enterprise than ivy leagues,
that dreams are too small
if there is not room enough for all.

Nobel winners must be servants
and Presidents as well.
Deliverance is a dream
that must be worked to tell.

Dr. King,
there is no millennium near,
but we are promising more
to more people in this land,
and my dream of President
is to work to deliver.

Finding Our Next Freedom High

Highs have come and gone for us.

Remembering how one grandmother looked
when thinking about her birth in freedom
and granddad's beginning during their war,
that quiet bringing distance into her eyes
with precious little speech.

Remembering the other grandmother
getting nervous to trembling in her red bone seat
when dad thanked two fathers
for love and meat at the kitchen table.

These women, hand maids of my upbringing
were married to and lived with Black men
born before that jubilee
or orphaned before losing all baby teeth.

They knew starting blocks of their husbands
and how announcements of emancipation
were voices thrown from hiding faces,
so they scrambled to keep doing miracles.

And then Mom,
who as child was brought from one South
to live in another above a moving line,
would smile at promises of a North place
after her hushed stories of lynching grace,
to keep me from searching
for a freedom high in geography.

Home Less

Remembering the dirty beard
that deviled my yellow face,
hair combed by angle of sleep,
soaked jeans from yellow rain,
tight hold of a church gallery,
light space between iron belly
of my sister's skyhawk,
the unforgiving concrete
of the church carport
and the shrinking green of a bush
in the parsonage yard
that left my feet exposed,

I was less homeless than now.

There were mirrors then to remind
I was not alone,
the cocked eyes of neighbors
that had seen me once in pulpits
or on ivy walls,
the bowed eyes of children
who had looked up before
at a hero's hope.

Even more clear was the view inside.

And yet,
with the host of underside company then,
the living moving filth
to which all ground is clean,
I was less homeless than now.

It is not living without a country
that keeps my hand out,

nor even the distant hands of those
who look like me
that know only to reach in,
but children who are too short to see.

There is no home without children,
without the spirit of breathing change,
without their fight against adult diseases,
without their belief that the best dreams
of long lives they have seen are possible.

Deep wounds of spirit
send the best to streets,
but growing pictures of sober children
dreaming against sleep
to be richly empty
leave me poor in memory,
without doors I know how to turn.

If these children have only slaveries
to remember,
we shall never be African again.

Leaving Prayer Meeting Early

Wednesday evening games were special.

Preacher's kid that I was,
I needed you there more than God,
no matter my position
to feel my best.

Tall boy at thirteen,
taller yet being your son,
I was raised by you
and new Black men in the majors.

You taught me how to pitch,
keep eyes on the ball till contact,
and believe I was good as the rest.

Heroes showed the skills
I had read each day in Negro newspapers,
and caught their mouths
as well as seamed circles.

Beaned so often by Whites
throwing straight at the heart,
they punched out mirrors
in the tenth inning
without stories of cracked glass,
and were loud after locker rooms closed.

When you left deacons in charge
of finding proper knees to look up
at the mid-week prayer meeting,
I looked up to you,
least because I was not as tall;
no matter what inning you

became part of the rough diamond,
final scores changed with your eyes,
for you reminded me
the ball and bat were always in my hands,
and I should worry less
about how the strikes were called.

I stay at prayer meetings now
often outside the church
to keep feet on the ground,
remembering dugout lessons you taught by example
there was no loss
if I looked back to see
worlds coming at me
and gave my best.

Daughters Striking Color

After the birth blow,
you were not struck by color.

You grabbed away ancestral brushes
with more browns than red bone
that left you somehow forgiving light,
and stroked in rich earth
for both beauty
and distance from white
in crushed fields and home.

Yours was never the old crippled match
of dark men sniffing yellow
with gold to buy new faces
for children to be born
fair enough to catch a climb.

Even as teenage girls,
with your grandfathers and me
kept in sprawling shade too long,
you both found sun in boys
sent smiles outside and in.

I wonder now
how my girls with Shirley Temple curls
but Black at heart
found their own beauty
beyond the color hated and loved.

This old man yet your father
needs to believe

the books you were required to read,
rituals of crinkled hair,
and my refusal to leave Black communities,
loving them in deed,
put the brush first in your hearts
to color freedom beyond skin.

Birth Days

Jackie Robinson fathered the man in Negro boys
who always loved their own leagues,
and whistling at white chalk markings
that lined out playing fields.

Preparing for the first Booker T. School
in a state run by white empty robes
that made all important rules,
that offered your dad millions of bills
if he would sign his only name
to support hoods running globes,

I picked up a light wooden Louisville slugger,
lifted it high slightly bent
to test circles in the sky
the way he hit the ball
on the round twelve-inch Admiral
in the store you bought my first glove.

This segregated start in sports
was before I saw you pick up the bat
from either side
and swing to level fences
for our family to survive.

I never learned to hit well enough
with the right eye closest to the ball
though I was more than tough
when I squared shoulders
with my weakest hand on top.

Continuing to push bats in the air
like the first Black in that major league,
needing the thick handle he used

to keep the fingers full of wooden weapon
to level playing fields,
it was you I followed singly
with your model of pitch and catch.

Only every ninth time you advised,
if then, would the bat be in my hands,
when as a pitcher I would deliver
each ball for as many innings
with no relief in sight.

So I have always tiptoed
at the top of the throw, bounced like you,
never left my eyes from the catcher's mitt,
bearing down with control,
finishing with balance to catch the hit.

You and Mr. Robinson were born
that eventful year of nineteen repeating self,
of wars abroad and riots here,
of a segregated capitol
and honoring of still birth of a nation
by a president from the south
and Ivy League education.

If I came from retirement for
the much smaller contest match,
I would worry less about hitting balls out of the park
three or four times a game
when a miss of pitch or catch
might mean the team would fall.

A hit will only raise one's average at the plate
but not be enough for the larger win.

Excuse Me! I Didn't See Anyone Else

A Black Night Manager at the front desk
assigned me to an elite floor at Marriott
in the home of country music.

Done with a knowing wink,
she showed me how to use the key,
hoping I enjoyed two days with rich folks.

At the restaurants both mornings at nine,
I noted the strut of small and old kids
who talked loudly about the tenth floor
with heads erect enough
for middle afternoon blaze of day.

Even the way dads signed room numbers
on the checks for their help
made me glad they were not company.

Finding the slot for entry to plastic worlds,
I rose to artificial heights again,
and felt my pocket for the hard slice
that would let me on easy street again.

Then there was the white maid voice
opening the occupied place next door,
followed by the white woman inside
peeking out to let me know when they'd leave
and I could clean the room at noon.

Knocking her back down with a practiced stare
for ancient scenes that won't go away,
I added I am Dr. Hord, and she
with no practice of apology, said,
Excuse me! I did not see anyone else.

Why would I be uppity enough
to flaunt a title on the tenth floor?
The President was Black, God was
wherever she asked Him to be,
and all else was right with the world.

Slave Ads Without the Wanted

Have you noticed Bill Russell's laugh
after his missing voice in the new Coors' ad?

Russell is not original,
is rather a sharp copy
of black men in the fields
who were tall enough
to look out for others
and too tall
to be caught alive shuffling.

Coors is not original,
is rather a light copy
of white men in the house
who made themselves short enough
to be blind beyond themselves,
to crouch from the high finger
pointed at their slavery.

The back side
of Russell's voice is gone.

In the tradition,
insisting on his own smile,
he stands up again
without echo,
and towers over those
who draw dry life now
from wet and quiet gutters.

Watching Blankets Move: An Early Eulogy

Even before you knew
milk was poison for me
and my tiny hands were tied
for scratching fire from my face,
father eyes watched small blankets
covering quiet parts of me
to be sure I was alive.

The first child,
you blinked fewer times
than on the long steel mill job
that paid black men a quarter an hour
when you labored near the basinet.

Whether a life disease beckoned my body
or I was in dark pink of health,
whether you were at end
of another thirteen hour day
or between extra segregated jobs,
you would never leave the room
till blankets kept moving with my heave.

Though I grew to beds your size,
your eyes stayed the vigil,
adding pride to my safety
till I no longer lay beneath skies
of your roof.

Now your rooms with lowered ceilings
are where I stand
as you lie under white sheets
that thin with sleeping,
and each time I cross the hold,
I look for signs you did
before I was a boy.

My job has less joy
for I cannot sustain you
with steady eyes
or long days at my mill.

Still, your old practice is now instinct,
and I am inside your place
even when outside your door,
watching always the gauze
your blankets have become.

Somehow,
each dream of you,
each painful trip
to your closing room
helps me to recognize
your blankets will move
long after my eyes are gone.

Your Eyes Have It: A Black Man Listens

You found the eyes to see my beauty.

It does not matter now
where you found them;

it does not matter how,
whether in the ancient books,
the pride of a generation ago,
your own living black
or all of those.

You found the eyes to see my beauty.

I know one grandmother was brown,
your mother was brown,
and all girls of your young loving
were loved by the sun.

But even with all that learning
and loving,
it seems the way you look at me
comes from another time and place.

My black face is more than beautiful
now that you have seen it,
and cannot hide the joy
when I am with you.

Your eyes have it.

AUG 0 1 2014